FINDING GOD

Compiled by
Louis M. Savary and
Thomas J. O'Connor

NEWMAN PRESS   *   NEW YORK   *   1971

Library of Congress Catalog Card Number: 73-133467
Book design and art work by Ragna Tischler Goddard
Coordinated by Donald F. Brophy
Published by Newman Press
Editorial Office: 304 W. 58th St., N.Y., N.Y. 10019
Business Office: Paramus, New Jersey 07652
Printed and bound in the United States of America

ACKNOWLEDGMENTS

The authors wish to thank Harper & Row, Publishers, for permission to reprint material by Schubert M. Ogden, Erich Fromm, and Herman Hesse; Dell Publishing Co. for the excerpt by Kurt Vonnegut, Jr., from *God Bless You, Mr. Rosewater*, © 1968, a Seymour Lawrence Book; Dial Press, Inc. for material by Norman Mailer from *An American Dream; America* for permission to reprint the poem by Denis Wiseman, from *America,* March 28, 1970, all rights reserved, © 1970, America Press Inc., 106 W. 56th St., N.Y., N.Y. 10019; Paulist-Newman Press for permission to reprint material by William L. Kelly, James Carroll, and Karl Rahner; *The Critic* for permission to use material by John Tracy Ellis, © 1970 by the Thomas More Association; *Theology Digest* for permission to reprint material by Hubert Reifenhauser, Jurgen Moltmann, and Emerich Coreth; Cheval-Stanyan Co. for permission to reprint poems by Rod McKuen; *Continuum* for permission to reprint material by Robert O. Johann and Philip Berrigan; Holt, Rinehart and Winston, Inc. for permission to reprint the excerpt from "Birches" by Robert Frost, from *The Poetry of Robert Frost* edited by Edward Connery Lathem, copyright 1916 © 1969 by Holt, Rinehart and Winston, Inc., copyright 1944 by Robert Frost, and for permission to reprint excerpts from *Chicago Poems* by Carl Sandburg, copyright 1916 by Holt, Rinehart and Winston, Inc., copyright 1944 by Carl Sandburg; Harcourt Brace Jovanovich, Inc., for permission to use material from *Wind, Sand and Stars* by Antoine de Saint-Exupery and from *The Third Revolution* by Karl Stern, and for permission to reprint three poems from *73 Poems* by E. E. Cummings, © 1963 by Marion Morehouse Cummings (the poem "who are you, little i" first appeared in *The New Yorker*); *Cross Currents* for permission to reprint an excerpt by Rosemary Ruether; the excerpts by Bernard Lonergan, © 1969 by Bernard Lonergan, also appeared first in *Cross Currents; Pace* magazine for permission to reprint material by Abraham H. Maslow; material by James L. Connor first appeared in *The Catholic Review;* New Directions for permission to reprint material from *Big Sur and the Oranges of Hieronymous Bosch* by Henry Miller, copyright © 1957 by New Directions Publishing Corporation, and for permission to use material from "I Am Waiting" by Lawrence Ferlinghetti, from *A Coney Island of the Mind,* copyright © 1958 by Lawrence Ferlinghetti; Doubleday & Company, Inc., for permission to reprint lines from "The Imperfect Eye," copyright © 1964 by John L'Heureux, from *Quick*

BELIEVING IN GOD

FAITH GIVES SUBSTANCE TO OUR HOPES AND MAKES us certain of realities we do not see (Hebrews 11:1). ❧ To find God, to believe in him, to affirm his reality and his meaning for human life—is this possible for today? ❧ There are those who want to believe, who would like to surrender themselves to God in faith, to yield to him their minds and hearts, like buds on a tree waiting to open itself to Spring. ❧ But for some belief in God is a question mark hanging in the cold air of a November day. They listen for signs of God and hear only the dull throbbing of their own heartbeats. ❧ There are those who knew God's presence when they were younger—perhaps long ago—but now have lost him. They say that they can no longer experience the divine. Once God seemed as close to them, as vivid, as the sun burning in the noonday skies—or close as footsteps in the forests of night. Once they knew the holy and felt the intensity of the sacred. But now they wander and wonder. Of God there is for them only remembering and hoping and waiting. ❧ For some, from whose world God seems absent, everything seems matter-of-fact and without color; food is tasteless, every sound is an irritating noise. Uncertainty echoes their every step along the empty road; in the fog, their eyes can barely see the light of the next street-lamp. Life for them has lost real meaning. ❧ While some still search for God, others who once tried have ceased to make the effort. Are their eyes alive—or are they cold and unmoving? ❧ Without God in their world, do they try to make something worthwhile of life—or are they people without hope and without dreams? Perhaps they are able to find some human meaning. Or perhaps the stone of this particular denial may have settled at the bottom of their hearts. Some may attempt to live a life of value and worth, to live for others. Others may feel dried up, exhausted, like empty masks on a stage, or solitary planets floating without direction in the void of space. ❧ But even the believer's life of faith is not a secure one. From time to time even he cries out, "I do not know." He reaches out for strength to others who share his desire to believe. But he feels God's absence as surely as the non-believer does. He can find no scheduled route to his destination. Each day he must search the evidence anew for signs of final meaning, signals of the transcendent. And each day he must practice dying. ❧ In the presence of the idea of God a believer may feel at times that he is only a shadow or that he is bouncing helplessly through an impossible world. He may feel he needs the certainty of faith, just to cope effectively with the details of everyday life. ❧ He may be for the most part sure he has found a secure path, yet still feel that each step is a prayer asking for the courage to believe. The believer must, in any case, weave his way through webs of myth and metaphor, symbol and cult. The behavior is always waiting, too, for God to speak his first new word, waiting for the insight to crackle like fresh fire from a charred ember, waiting to be made alive again!

11

A DESPERATE YEARNING

In an age of supposed unbelief
people are yearning in a desperate way
for something to believe in.
Their nakedly exposed need
is openly shared.
The institutions of organized religion
have, they feel, frustrated
and betrayed this yearning again and again.
These are the reasons for the summons we now hear.

Malcolm Boyd

AN APPEAL FOR TRANSFORMATION

I appeal to you, therefore, brethren,
by the mercies of God,
to present your bodies
as a living sacrifice,
holy and acceptable to God,
the worship offered by mind and heart.
Adapt yourselves no longer
to the pattern of this present world,
but let your minds be remade
and your whole nature thus transformed.
Then you will be able
to discern the will of God,
and to know what is good,
acceptable, and perfect.

Romans 12:1-2

THE DEEPEST DENIAL

The crucial point is that unfaith, like faith,
is a phenomenon occurring
at two essentially different levels of human life.
At the deepest level . . .
it is, one may say, an atheism
in the bottom of the heart,
instead of an atheism
in the top of the mind . . .
One may affirm God's reality with one's mind
as well as one's lips,
and yet deny his reality
by actually existing as a godless man.

Schubert M. Ogden

YOU DO NOT ASK QUESTIONS

Old Beaucrat, my comrade,
it is not you who are to blame.
No one ever helped you to escape.
You, like the termite, built your peace
by blocking up with cement
every chink and cranny
through which the light might pierce.
You rolled yourself up into a ball
in your genteel security, in routine,
in the stifling convention of provincial life,
raising a modest rampart
against the winds and the tides and the stars.
You have chosen not to be perturbed
by our great problems,
have trouble enough to forget
your faith as a man.

You are not a dweller
upon an errant planet
and do not ask yourself questions
to which there are no answers . . .
Nobody grasped you by the shoulder
while there was still time.
Now the clay of which you were shaped
has dried and hardened,
and not in you will ever awaken
the sleeping musician,
the poet, the astronomer
that possibly inhabited you
from the beginning.

Antoine de Saint-Exupery

"YOU'VE GOT TO BE KIND"

"Congratulate Mary Moody on her twins."
"I will. I'll be baptizing them tomorrow."
"Baptizing?" This was something new . . . "I—I didn't
know you—you did things like that," said Sylvia carefully . . .
"I couldn't get out of it," said Eliot. "She insisted
on it, and nobody else would do it."
"Oh." Sylvia relaxed . . .
"I told her," said Eliot, . . . "that I wasn't a religious
person by any stretch of the imagination. I told her nothing
I did would count in Heaven, but she insisted just the same."
"What will you say? What will you do?"
"Oh—I don't know." Eliot's sorrow and exhaustion
dropped away for a moment as he became enchanted by the
problem. A birdy little smile played over his lips. "Go
over to her shack, I guess. Sprinkle some water on the
babies, say 'Hello, babies. Welcome to Earth. It's hot
in the summer and cold in the winter. It's round and wet
and crowded. At the outside, babies, you've got about a
hundred years here. There's only one rule that I know of,
babies—:
" 'God damn it, you've got to be kind.' "

Kurt Vonnegut, Jr.

An Idea of God and the Devil

"I don't know, Steve, it's not good to think too much—at least the way I do. Cause I always end up with something like the idea that God is weaker because I didn't turn out well."

"You don't believe everything is known before it happens?"

"Oh, no. Then there's no decent explanation for evil. I believe God is just doing His best to learn from what happens to some of us. Sometimes I think He knows less than the Devil because we're not good enough to reach Him. So the Devil gets most of the best messages we think we're sending up."

Norman Mailer

TYGER, TYGER

Tyger, Tyger, burning bright
In the forests of the night,
What immortal hand or eye
Could frame thy fearful symmetry?

In what distant deeps or skies
Burnt the fire of thine eyes?
On what wings dare he aspire?
What the hand dare seize the fire?

And what shoulder and what art
Could twist the sinews of thy heart?
And, when thy heart began to beat,
What dread hand and what dread feet?

What the hammer? What the chain?
In what furnace was thy brain?
What the anvil? What dread grasp
Dare its deadly terrors clasp?

When the stars drew down their spears,
And watered heaven with their tears,
Did He smile his work to see?
Did He who made the lamb make thee?

Tyger, Tyger, burning bright
In the forests of the night,
What immortal hand or eye
Dare frame thy fearful symmetry?

William Blake

YOUR VOICE

Your voice
from the past
is carved in my bark,
defining me forever
as tree
growing old
around your words.

Denis Wiseman

BOTH KINDS OF ELEMENTS

By the continual living activity
of its non-rational elements
a religion is guarded
from passing into "rationalism."
By being steeped in
and saturated with rational elements
it is guarded from sinking
into fanaticism or mere mysticality . . .

Rudolf Otto

"TAKE AWAY THIS CUP . . ."

And he said to them,
"My soul is very sorrowful,
even to death;
remain here, and watch."
And going a little farther,
he fell on the ground
and prayed that, if it were possible,
the hour might pass from him.
And he said, "Abba, Father,
all things are possible to you;
take away this cup from me;
yet not what I will,
but what you will."

Mark 14:34-36

RUNNING AWAY FROM GOD

O Lord, I have been running away from you
the whole day long.
I have sought refuge in my work
and have let myself be driven
by the business of the day.
I have gone my way—without you.
Still you have followed me.
In all that I did, you were near at hand.
You were looking at me,
even when I wanted to hide.
You heard my every word—
yes, even those which were not intended
for your ears.
Even my most secret thoughts
were open to you.

William L. Kelly

THIRST FOR GOD

As a hart longs for flowing streams,
so longs my soul for thee, O God.
My soul thirsts for God, for the living God.
When shall I come and behold the face of God?
My tears have been my food day and night,
while men say to me continually, "Where is your God?"
These things I remember, as I pour out my soul:
how I went with the throng,
and led them in procession to the house of God,
with glad shouts and songs of thanksgiving,
a multitude keeping festival.
Why are you cast down, O my soul,
and why are you disquieted within me?
Hope in God; for I shall again praise him,
my help and my God.

Psalm 42:1-5

"HELP MY UNBELIEF"

The cure of some aspects
of the Church's present malaise
must be discovered
in Winston Churchill's words:
in "blood, toil, tears and sweat" . . .
They must cultivate sophistication
in what pertains to their religious faith
by reconciling themselves
with the simple declaration,
"I do not know."
The revolution through which the Church is now passing
has been variously described as a crisis in relevance,
a crisis in authority,
and a crisis in identity.
Are these not really different expressions
of what constitutes the heart of the matter,
namely, a crisis in faith?
To say, therefore, in answer to many
of the tormenting questions of the present hour,
"I do not know,"
is not to contribute to the pervading agnosticism
and atheism of our time.
It is rather to take the first step
toward a firm renewal of faith
after the model of the distraught father
who sought Jesus' cure for his son
bedeviled by an evil spirit.
"Lord, I do believe," he said, "help my unbelief."

John Tracy Ellis

35

THE GOD QUESTION

In the spiritual situation of man today,
the God question has not disappeared
but has surfaced in another spot.
The God question expresses
man's search for his final
goal of meaning,
his own self-understanding,
and for the final orientation
which covers and embraces
all his necessary daily activities . . .

Hubert Reifenhäuser

SEEING WHAT IS GOOD

Who among us has not suddenly
looked into his child's face,
in the midst of the toils
and troubles of everyday life,
and at that moment "seen"
that everything which is good,
is loved and lovable,
loved by God!

Josef Pieper

MAY 26

I'd rather be without a woman
than know a God I couldn't trust.
That's why I pray with caution
till I'm sure.

I gave myself to myself only
for so long a time
I've had to be led back
to God and women too,
step
by
step.

Now halfway home
it's time I knelt down
on the asphalt once again
and prayed for more than daily bread.

Rod McKuen

I COMMITTED MYSELF TO HIM

The day after my conversion I went into the hay-field
to lend a hand with the harvest,
and not having made any promise to God to abstain
I took too much and came home drunk.
I felt ashamed of myself, but I knew
that God's work begun in me was not going to be wasted.

About midday I made on my knees
the first prayer before God for twenty years.
I did not ask to be forgiven;
I felt that was no good.
Well, what did I do?
I committed myself to him in the profoundest belief
that my individuality was going to be destroyed,
that he would take all from me,
and I was willing.
In such a surrender lies the secret of a holy life . . .

Since I gave up to God all ownership in my own life,
he has guided me in a thousand ways,
and has opened my path in a way almost incredible
to those who do not enjoy the blessing
of a truly surrendered life.

Anon. Oxford Graduate

ORIENTATION AND CONFIDENCE

A person can confidently attend
to the details and concerns of everyday life
only when his large-scale orientation
and adjustment to his surroundings
are a matter of routine . . .

Robert O. Johann

I'D LIKE TO GET AWAY AWHILE

It's when I'm weary of considerations,
And life is too much like a pathless wood
Where your face burns and tickles with the cobwebs
Broken across it, and one eye is weeping
From a twig's having lashed across it open.
I'd like to get away from earth awhile
And then come back to it and begin over.
May no fate willfully misunderstand me
And half grant what I wish and snatch me away
Not to return. Earth's the right place for love:
I don't know where it's likely to go better.
I'd like to go by climbing a birch tree,
And climb black branches up a snow-white trunk
Toward heaven, till the tree could bear no more,
But dipped its top and set me down again.
That would be good both going and coming back.
One could do worse than be a swinger of birches.

Robert Frost

 PRAYER OF DAVID

But who am I,
and what is my people,
that we should be able
thus to offer willingly?
For all things come from you,
and of your own have we given you.
For we are strangers before you,
and sojourners,
as all our fathers were;
our days on the earth
are like a shadow,
and there is no abiding.
O Lord our God,
all this abundance
that we have provided
for building you a house
for your holy name
comes from your hand
and is all your own.

I Chronicles 29:14-16

PRAYER AND BELIEF

Praying helps us to have the courage to believe,
and belief is demanded of each one of us.

Karl Rahner

LOST

Desolate and lone
All night long on the lake
Where fog trails and mist creeps,
The whistle of a boat
Calls and cries unendingly,
Like some lost child
In tears and trouble
Hunting the harbor's breast
And the harbor's eyes.

Carl Sandburg

BELIEVING IMPOSSIBLE THINGS

The Queen remarked . . . "Now I'll give you something to believe. I'm just one hundred and one, five months and a day."

"I can't believe that!" said Alice.

"Can't you?" the Queen said in a pitying tone. "Try again: Draw a long breath, and shut your eyes."

Alice laughed. "There's no use trying," she said: "One can't believe impossible things."

"I daresay you haven't had much practice," said the Queen. "When I was your age, I always did it for half-an-hour a day. Why, sometimes I believed as many as six impossible things before breakfast."

Lewis Carroll

TO TRUST WHOLLY IN GOD

So then let [the soul]
of its very necessity
make the venture
to trust wholly and completely
in the Lord God.
In this very way
the soul is so pleasing to God,
that he bestows his own grace upon it,
and by that very grace
it comes to feel the true love and affection
which drives away all doubt
and all fear
and hopes confidently in God.

Martin Luther

ON DARKNESS

End of the chapter, drop the book,
slide under the sheets, draw up the spread.
Poised on an elbow, pound the pillow,
stretch for the button that turns
the darkness on and the silence.
The pillow is briefly hollow like some ocean.
The whole room breathes in the blackness.
Stillness at last, no earnest echoes,
words or creaking smiles, none
of the shouted love, whispered hate.
The dark's only sound is the clapping
of its one free hand as day
wrecks itself on night in me.
Warm, yet I shudder and slide further down.
Tired, yet I clench the pillow closer,
Dark, yet I squeeze my eyes out of light.
I push my feet away, stretch at the knees
and will my bodied mind asleep.
All in vain, for the moment is come
and I know again that I am alone.

James Carroll

FINDING GOD WITHIN

A LL THAT CAME TO BE WAS alive with his life; that life was the light of men (John 1:4). ❦ God is discovered within. A shadow is taken from the eyes, a heart of stone is transformed. The lonely person seems no longer alone, no longer lost, no longer without meaning. The person who seems to have lost the power to love comes alive again and his hand reaches out to touch a new face. ❦ The Spirit penetrates where there had been no room for God. The infection of mistrust is healed, guilty hearts are made clean, bodies and spirits are washed with pure water and strengthened with the fire of God. ❦ To find God within, is to find warmth and assurance at creation's source. Silent listening is possible; belonging is possible; love is possible. Man is no longer alone, no longer empty and hollow. He can walk in hope. He can sense God's presence. Sunlight and daily work, the kitchen and the basement, the piano, a child's doll, all have a basis in meaning now. In the stifling and bewildering world, a person may listen for the Spirit's special word about his human life, children, jobs, hopes, responsibilities and disappointments. ❦ The Spirit brings calmness and confidence. Purpose flows through the world of complexity. The new and unknown no longer threaten. They are swept into the current of life, and a strong man or woman may dance in its river. ❦ God invites people to become aware of themselves—of the meaning and value of their personal lives. In his own liberty God makes himself known within the minds and spirits of his people, setting them free to follow their own deepest desires. Shattered hopes are pieced together. Torn threads of dreams are rewoven. The fabric of fresh ideals is fashioned upon a frame of freedom and confidence. ❦ A person is made new in mind and spirit and puts on a new nature of God's making. A mannequin is transformed into flesh. The flesh is given new life, a new center of orientation. It is the revolution of being born again.

# A SIGN FROM GOD

Again the Lord spoke to Ahaz,
"Ask a sign of the Lord your God;
let it be deep as Sheol
or high as heaven."
But Ahaz said, "I will not ask,
and I will not put the Lord to the test."
And he said, "Hear then, O house of David!
Is it too little for you to weary men,
that you weary my God also?
Therefore the Lord himself
will give you a sign.
Behold, a young woman shall conceive
and bear a son,
and shall call his name Emmanuel.
He shall eat curds and honey
when he knows how to refuse the evil
and choose the good . . ."

Isaiah 7:11-15

GOOD NEWS

And the angel said to them
"Be not afraid;
for behold, I bring you good news
of a great joy which will come to all the people;
for to you is born this day in the city of David
a Savior, who is Christ the Lord.
And this will be a sign for you:
you will find a babe wrapped in swaddling clothes
and lying in a manger."
And suddenly there was with the angel
a multitude of the heavenly host
praising God and saying
"Glory to God in the highest,
and on earth peace
among men with whom he is pleased!"

Luke 2:10-14

A CHILD'S HEART

The hearts of small children
are delicate organs.
A cruel beginning in this world
can twist them into curious shapes.
The heart of a child can shrink
so that forever afterward
it is hard and pitted
as the seed of a peach.
Or again, the heart of such a child
may fester and swell
until it is a misery to carry
within the body,
easily chafed and hurt
by the most ordinary things.

Carson McCullers

WHAT IT MEANS TO BE BORN

There are numerous examples to indicate
that the mere act of being born
is associated with anxiety.
To leave the sheltering womb,
to change from the passivity
of placental nourishment
to the act of breathing
is a tremendous revolution.
The first breath we breathe
is associated with primeval anxiety.
Being born means accepting
something new and unknown
and leaving security irretrievably behind.
Here, too, there exists
a continuum of images
from the primeval carnal experience,
which we all share,
to thousands of other forms of being born.

Karl Stern

NOT CUCKOO . . .

Do not hatch my eggs;
Sit on your own.
Once when I was younger
I poured out my troubles
To a teacher who said,
Do you know what that is?
That's pure Freud.
And I said, Well,
The hell it is!
That was pure me.
I have no desire
Now or ever
To hatch anyone else's eggs.
Not yours or Freud's or anyone's eggs
While I have eggs of my own.

Ione Hill

"I CAN'T HELP CRYING OUT"

Help me, Jesus.
I am Malcolm, alone.
Underneath a number of titles,
roles, functions and images—
this is who I am.
In this moment,
I find myself
asking deep and painful questions
about life.
I can't help crying out
in a world in which complexity
and feeling lost
seem to be more and more of a reality.

Malcolm Boyd

THE NEARNESS OF GOD

God is nearer to us than we are to ourselves.

St. Augustine

THE AMBIGUITY OF HUMAN LOVE

Human love can be ambiguous;
we do not know
whether it is safe to give
and to accept love.
It is a risk both to love and accept love,
and all of us to some degree
are afraid to take the risk.

Human fellowship is both heroic and tragic;
it is both renewing and destructive;
it is both healing and hurtful,
but it is indispensable to life.
This is our human predicament.

Something is needed to cut
into the ambiguity of human love.
This is what Christ does.
He draws the confused currents of human love
into the unifying stream of Divine love,
thus making possible a new relationship.

Reuel L. Howe

THE EXPERIENCE OF DISAPPOINTMENT

Few people escape the fate
that at one point or another in their development
their hopes are disappointed—
sometimes completely shattered.
Perhaps this is good.
If a man did not experience
the disappointment of his hope,
how could his hope
become strong and unquenchable?
How could he avoid the danger
of being an optimistic dreamer?

Erich Fromm

THE EVERYDAY HERO

To be a hero for a moment, for an hour,
is easier than to bear
the heroism of everyday life.
Accept life as it is—
gray and monotonous,
that activity for which no one praises you,
that heroism which no one notes,
which draws no attention to yourself.
He who bears the colorless challenge of life
and still remains a man
is indeed a hero!

Feodor Dostoevsky

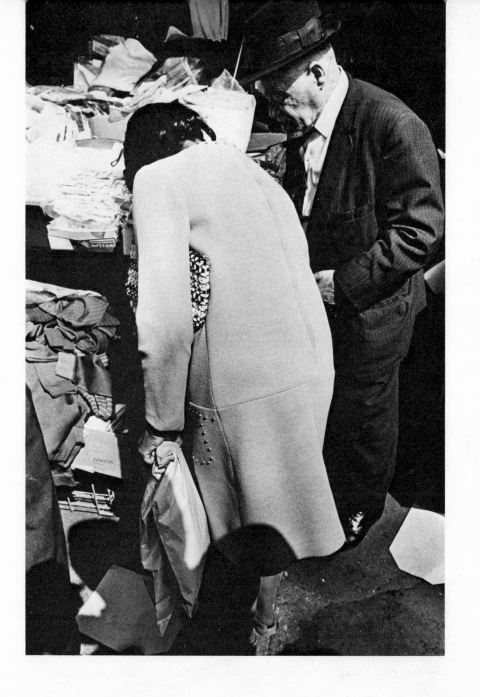

INSIGHT

Wandering through the cranberry patches
with a casual crowd of idle lads,
and fishing beneath bridges with the noise
of trains thundering above your head,
joking, throwing your shirt off in the grass,
and diving in high from the river-bank,
with one sudden thought, how little I
have done in life, how much I can do.

Yevtushenko

WHEN A REVELATION TAKES PLACE

Our understanding of God
is never achieved once and for all.
Our view of God remains always
through a glass, darkly.
However, something happens to a person
when revelation takes place,
and this we can see.
There is a new evaluation
of what he calls *good*.
There is a change
in the center of his orientation.
He sees things
"in a different light."
What the changes are can never be predicted,
but they can be seen and understood
after they occur.

William F. Fore

THIS SPARK SPEAKS TO YOU

And why does it make you sad
to see how everything hangs
by such thin and whimsical threads?
Because you're a dreamer,
an incredible dreamer,
with a tiny spark hidden
somewhere inside you
which cannot die,
which even you cannot kill or quench
and which tortures you horribly
because all the odds
are against its continual burning.
In the midst of the foulest decay
and putrid savagery,
this spark speaks to you
of beauty, of human warmth and kindness,
of goodness, of greatness,
of heroism, of martyrdom,
and it speaks to you of love.

Eldridge Cleaver

WHAT IS MAN?

What is man that you should think of him,
And the son of man that you should care for him?

Psalm 8:5

THE SOFTEST STUFF

The softest of stuff in the world
Penetrates quickly the hardest;
Insubstantial, it enters
Where no room is.

Lao Tzu

11

humble one (gifted with

illimitable joy)
bird sings love's every truth

beyond all since and why

asking no favor but

 (while down come blundering
proud hugenesses of hate

sometimes called world) to sing

e. e. cummings

TO SEE THE WORLD SHINE

I slept deeply until late in the morning.
The new day dawned for me like a solemn feast,
the kind I had not experienced since childhood.
I was full of a great restlessness,
yet without fear of any kind.
I felt that an important day had begun for me
and I saw and experienced the changed world around me,
expectant, meaningful, and solemn;
even the gentle autumn rain had its beauty
and a calm and festive air
full of happy, sacred music.
For the first time the outer world
was perfectly attuned to the world within;
it was a joy to be alive.
No house, no shop window, no face disturbed me,
everything was as it should be,
without any of the flat, humdrum look of the everyday;
everything was a part of Nature,
expectant and ready to face its destiny with reverence.

Hermann Hesse

BEING BORN ANEW

Jesus answered him, Truly, truly,
I say to you, unless one is born anew,
he cannot see the kingdom of God.
Nicodemus said to him,
How can a man be born when he is old?
Can he enter a second time
into his mother's womb
and be born?
Jesus answered, Truly, truly,
I say to you, unless one is born
of water and the Spirit,
he cannot enter the kingdom of God.
That which is born of the flesh
is flesh,
and that which is born of the Spirit
is spirit.
Do not marvel that I said to you,
"You must be born anew."
The wind blows where it wills,
and you hear the sound of it,
but you do not know whence it comes
or whither it goes;
so it is with everyone
who is born of the Spirit.

John 3:3-8

ACTING WITH CONVICTION

Let us do all things
in the conviction that He dwells in us.
Thus we shall be His temples
and He will be our God within us.
And this is the truth,
and it will be made manifest
before our eyes.
Let us, then, love Him as He deserves.

Ignatius of Antioch

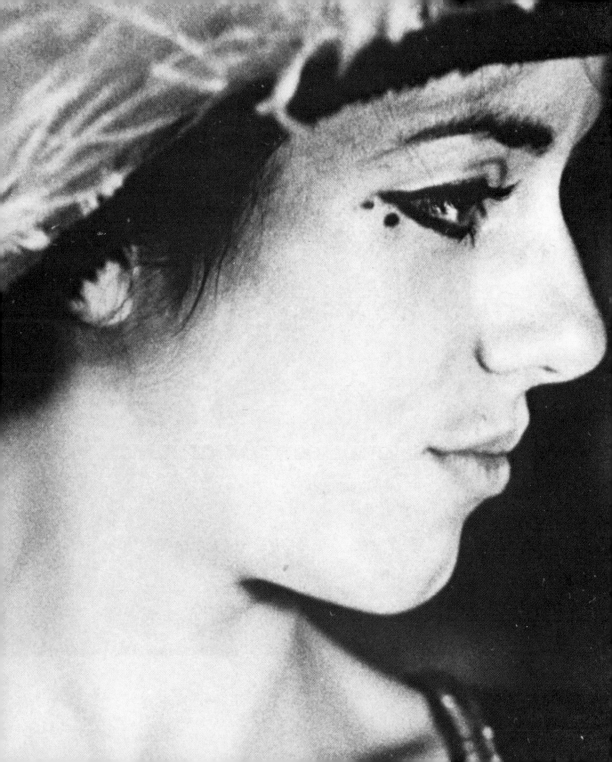

THE UPBUILDING OF THE PERSONAL

In a world of commerce
where the soul becomes lonely,
faith must address itself
to the inner existence of modern man
and provide meaning and direction
for personal life.
It must create for the inside
what is missing on the outside:
warmth, security,
receptivity, transcendence.

Jürgen Moltmann

LIGHT FOR TODAY

What does it matter, O Lord, if the future is dark?
To pray now for tomorrow—I am not able.
Keep my heart only for today, give me your protection
today, grant me your light—just for today.

Theresa of the Child Jesus

AUTHENTIC LOVE

But the love of God is not restricted
to particular areas of human beings . . .
It is also something in itself,
something personal, intimate and profoundly attuned
to the deepest yearnings of the human heart.
It constitutes a basic fulfilment of man's being.
Because it is such a fulfilment,
it is the source of a great peace,
the peace that the world cannot give.
It is a wellspring of joy that can endure
despite the sorrow of failure, humiliation,
privation, pain, desertion.
Because it is such a fulfilment,
it removes the temptation of all that is shallow,
hollow, empty and degrading,
without handing man over to the fanaticism . . .

Bernard Lonergan

THE PRESENCE OF GOD

We were on our sixth day of hiking, and in good shape.
I felt neither fatigue, hunger, nor thirst,
and my state of mind was equally healthy,
and there was not a shadow of uncertainty
about the road we should follow.

All at once I experienced a feeling
of being raised above myself.
I felt the presence of God—
I tell of the thing just as I was conscious of it—
as if his goodness and his power were penetrating me altogether.
The throb of emotion was so violent
that I could hardly tell the boys to pass on
and not wait for me.
I sat down on a stone,
unable to stand any longer,
and my eyes overflowed with tears.
I thanked God that in the course of my life
he had taught me to know him.
I begged him ardently that my life be consecrated
to the doing of his will.

Anonymous Swiss Writer

I AM WITH YOU

I am the Lord God of Abraham your father,
and the God of Isaac.
The land upon which you stand
I will give to you and to your seed.
And in you and in your seed
all the families of the earth shall be blessed.
And behold I am with you,
and will keep you in all the places that you go,
and will bring you again into this land.
For I will not leave you
until I have done what I have spoken of to you.

Genesis 28:13-15

MILES OF JOY

God, in our worried hearts we hide often from You
and from each other in old anxieties.
We forget that smiles at all the simple joys
are the surest signs of your being here.
You have given us a world full of children
and a night-time full of laughing stars.
The message is so simple we may miss it;
You are here in all of our everything:
in relief at windows hit and still unbroken,
in arguments ended at last in embracing,
in happy shocks of understanding between men.
Remind us, Lord, with strange seizures of joy
that these hates and wars and widowed hearts,
these moans of our time are exceptional.
Remind us, Lord, with ordinary happiness
that You have overcome all worlds of grief
and even now are wrapping us in coats
of common daily happenings of goodness.
Strip us, Lord, of melancholy strangeness,
for we accept your word, not that misery
is unreal or painless, but that all of life
is quick, shot through with You and therefore,
fundamentally, with miles and smiles of joy.

James Carroll

IN THE BURDEN OF FREEDOM

The ultimate, absolute principle
of all responsibility
is called God.
That silent listening
for what we ought to do
is a listening to God.

Karl Rahner

3 AUGUST

Been reading. Books I've read before.
Relaxed. The test of manhood.
Again. In Franny and Zooey have found
a more graceful measure of maturity. If
there must be a measure at all.
Salinger offers this: "A man should
be able to lie at the bottom of a hill with
his throat cut, slowly bleeding to death,
and if a pretty girl or an old woman should
pass by with a beautiful jug balanced perfectly
on the top of her head, he should be able to
rise himself up on one arm and see the jug
safely over the top of the hill."

Someone so at ease with his existence, with
an appreciation of beauty that intrudes even the
unique sensibilities of death, needs to judge
himself by no other criteria. It will do for me.

Richard Gooding

GOD AND MEANING

Many today
live out of a profound
and genuine faith,
and they experience
in this faith
a meaning that permeates
their whole life.
God is their absolute
ground of meaning . . .
they know from
internal experience
that if anything has meaning,
God has,
and everything else
has meaning only from him.
A new world of understanding
is formed out of faith in God,
who as the ground of meaning
lends meaning
to every experience.

Emerich Coreth

BELONGING TO THE LORD

No one of us lives,
and equally
no one of us dies,
for himself alone.
If we live,
we live for the Lord;
and if we die,
we die for the Lord.
Whether therefore
we live or die,
we belong
to the Lord.

Romans 14:7-8

THE MOTHER OF MOSES

And the daughter of Pharaoh came down to wash
herself at the river; and her maidens walked along
by the river's side; and when she saw the ark among the flags,
she sent her maid to fetch it. And when she had opened it,
she saw the child: and, behold, the baby wept.
And she had compassion on him, and said, "This is one of the
Hebrews' children." Then said his sister to Pharaoh's daughter,
"Shall I go and call a nurse of the Hebrew women,
that she may nurse the child for you?"
And Pharaoh's daughter said to her, "Go." And the maid went
and called the child's mother. And Pharaoh's daughter said unto her,
"Take this child, and nurse it for me, and I will give
you your wages." And the woman took the child, and nursed it.

Exodus 2:5-9

A NEW PEOPLE

I will sprinkle clean water upon you,
and you shall be clean from all your uncleannesses,
and from all your idols I will cleanse you.
A new heart I will give you,
and a new spirit I will put within you,
and I will take out of your flesh
the heart of stone
and give you a heart of flesh.
And I will put my spirit within you,
and cause you to walk in my statutes
and be careful to observe my ordinances.
You shall dwell in the land
which I gave to your fathers;
and you shall be my people,
and I will be your God.

Ezekiel 36:25-28

FINDING GOD EVERYWHERE

B Y FAITH WE PERCEIVE THAT THE UNIVERSE was fashioned by the word of God, so that the visible came forth from the invisible (Hebrews 11:3). ❦ Once God is present within, a new century begins. The world changes its skin, a new geography has to be charted, new libraries wait to be written. Old structures that have served their purpose break down, while new doors and windows open up, and God is found in all the things that have been made. ❦ Lions and flowers, typewriters and television sets, streets and flowerpots: The inward eye is opened and sees everything new, under the light of the Spirit. Every point on earth is equally near the divine. ❦ Winter is melting and everything seems fresh and holy. The sky rains down righteousness and the thirsty soil opens itself to God's grace. And salvation begins to rise up from within the earth, like blades of grass or the first flower. There is a passion for experience, a longing to see and touch things, to meet the whole world with love. This world seems to become ever more rich and personal. ❦ Most of all, to the person who searches for God everywhere, the world is a challenge. It is a mixture of paradoxes: a sanctuary where values are in upheaval, a place

where strong moral concern meets human indifference. Where coopera-
tion confronts competition. Here the beauty men have made stands along-
side the ugliness worked by those same human hands. Through these streets
walk the poet and the profligate, the giant and the delinquent. ❧ Yet to look
for God everywhere is to learn that men and women inhabit an earth which
has opportunities as well as problems. It is an earth which might in this
generation explode into fragments—or move toward a new center. ❧ Man
today faces a crucial decision. He can choke to death in his own smoke and
fire. Or he can emerge, one with nature and creation, on the shore of a new
ocean. ❧ Standing for the first time at the tideline he may dare at first only
to pick up driftwood or pebbles along the shore. Soon he may find himself
shaping the wet sand with his hand and walking to the edge of the surf.
Then he may test the water, and then perhaps swim. Everywhere he turns,
in everything he touches, he may discover something about God. The believer who allows himself to be enveloped by God can smile, can laugh,
can cry with happiness. The old order has passed. All things are new. The
kingdom of God is at hand.

HIS PURPOSE IN DYING

The love of Christ leaves us no choice,
when once we have reached the conclusion
that one man died for all
and therefore all mankind has died.
His purpose in dying for all
was that men, while still in life,
should cease to live for themselves,
and should live for him
who for their sake died
and was raised to life . . .
When anyone is united to Christ,
there is a new world;
the old order has gone,
and a new order has already begun.

2 Corinthians 5:14-17

BEGINNING ANYWHERE

I feel as if there are apples
bursting out on every branch simultaneously.
It's as if you have got to pick
a million apples all at the same time,
and you can go to any branch,
you can go to any institution.
Just set me going! And it's fun.
You can spend a whole lifetime
just on transforming journalism, for example.
And the day you die
you can look back and say
it was a good life.
Go into any branch of any profession—
politics, religion, anything.
You can start
applying these principles, figuring out,
"If this is so, then what will be the consequences?"
This is one century confronting another;
the beginning of a new century of work.

Abraham H. Maslow

# A NEW SKIN

Faith is a man's response to God,
and this changes from age to age
because man is conditioned by his culture . . .
The world needs a new skin.
The old one has become too tight
for the realities of these times.

James L. Connor

JANUARY 11

I dare not think what might replace
the shadows that I've had to learn to love,
but I stand ready one more time
to learn a new geography
if that becomes a necessary thing to do.

Rod McKuen

LIMITS TO PARADISE

The windows of the soul are infinite, we are told . . .
If there are any flaws in your paradise,
open more windows! . . .
Open and alert, it matters little
whether one finds a supposed short cut to the Indies
or discovers a new world.
Everything is begging to be discovered,
not accidentally, but intuitively.
Seeking intuitively,
one's destination is never in a beyond of time or space
but always here and now.
One's destination is never a place
but rather a new way of looking at things.
There are no limits to paradise.
Any paradise worth the name
can sustain all the flaws in creation
and remain undiminished, untarnished . . .
In a paradise you don't teach or preach.
You practice the perfect life—
or you relapse.

Henry Miller

ROADS OF POSSIBILITY

As Ernst Bloch puts it,
"Man is he who is not yet" . . .
The kingdom of God stands as a symbol . . .
It is also a present power
working in history from beyond,
drawing men out of their small, self-enclosed Egypts
where they have become enslaved
and setting their feet on the road
out into the desert insecurity
and toward ever new promised lands.
The person who is especially delegated
to shake the people out of their old structures
and get them back on the road
toward new vistas
is the prophet.

Rosemary Ruether

To Know the Lord

And no longer
shall each man
teach his neighbor
and each his brother,
saying,
"Know the Lord,"
for they shall all
know me,
from the least of them
to the greatest,
says the Lord;
for I will forgive
their iniquity,
and I will
remember their sin
no more.

Jeremiah 31:34

THE CHRISTIAN AS REVOLUTIONARY

The Christian, then, by rebirth and constitution,
is a revolutionary . . .
And like his Lord,
he lives the conviction
that in a liveable society—just and human—
social order will come through the poor—
not Marx's proletariat or the materially poor,
but rather those who divest themselves
of even their human rights,
who are in effect,
interested only
in the rights of the brother.
"We have passed out of death and into life,
and of this we can be sure
because we love our brothers" (1 John 3:14).

Philip Berrigan

Too Self-Sufficient

We have forgotten the gracious hand
which preserved us in peace,
and multiplied and strengthened us;
and we have vainly imagined,
in the deceitfulness of our hearts,
that all these blessings were produced
by some superior wisdom or virtue
of our own.
Intoxicated with unbroken successes,
we have become too self-sufficient
to feel the necessity
of redeeming and preserving grace,
too proud to pray to the God
that made us.

Abraham Lincoln

HAPPINESS

I asked professors who teach the meaning of life to tell me what is happiness.
And I went to famous executives who boss the work of thousands of men.
They all shook their heads and gave me a smile as though I was trying to fool with them.
And then one Sunday afternoon I wandered out along the Desplaines river
And I saw a crowd of Hungarians under the trees with their women and children and a keg of beer and an accordion.

Carl Sandburg

114

GOD IN MAN

Man is suffering
and God is lost in him.

John L'Heureux

NOT UNTIL THEN

Not until a man has become so utterly unhappy,
or has grasped the woefulness of life so deeply
that he is moved to say, and mean it:
life for me has no value—
not until then is he able to make a bid for Christianity.
And then his life may acquire the very highest value.

Soren Kierkegaard

WORD OF CAUTION . . .

Look, but consider well
Before you touch a living thing:
You may think to put it back
But you cannot put it back
Unchanged, once you've touched it.
So what you see then
Is not what you might have seen;
Look well before you touch
With word or hand
A living thing.

Ione Hill

63

(listen)

this a dog barks and
how crazily houses
eyes people smiles
faces streets
steeples are eagerly

tumbl

ing through wonder
ful sunlight
—look—
selves, stir: writhe
o-p-e-n-i-n-g

are (leaves; flowers) dreams

, come quickly come
run run
with me now
jump shout (laugh
dance cry

sing) for it's Spring

—irrevocably;
and in
earth sky trees
:every
where a miracle arrives

(yes)

e. e. cummings

HYACINTHS TO FEED THE SOUL

If of thy mortal goods
thou art bereft,
And from thy slender store two
loaves alone to thee are left,
Sell one, and with the dole
Buy hyacinths to feed thy soul.

Muslih-uddin Sadi

That poem taught me a good deal . . .
I've made a hobby of noticing people
and whether or not they know
about using non-essentials and extravagances
occasionally
to feed the soul.
The happiest people do.

Carol Amen

FILLED WITH GOOD THINGS

We give you thanks, O God, for orange juice,
for chevrolets, for grandchildren in the sun,
for mere glances between daughters and men,
for a thousand amber miles of summertime.
We give you thanks for these six tall feet,
for seventy years, for that nameless center
that points us toy-boat-like to you.
We give you thanks, O God, for mud pies
and for the great delight of sharing them,
of showing them to passing strangers,
for the joy of confiding our mud together.
We give you thanks for carter's ink
and all the easy things we daily use
and never think about or notice.
We thank you for the alphabet and most
especially for the marvelous letter 'Z'
which, like ourselves, looks so pointed
and painful, but given chance to show itself
is easy, soft, lazy, slightly secret.

James Carroll

A FOLLOWER OF JESUS

If anyone wishes to be a follower of mine,
he must leave self behind;
he must take up his cross
and come with me.
Whoever cares for his own safety is lost;
but if a man will let himself be lost
for my sake,
he will find his true self.
What will a man gain
by winning the whole world,
at the cost of his true self?

Matthew 16:24-26

THE SKIER

For two or three days before a race,
I'm trying to get a lot of rest.
I'm not soaking in the bathtub too long,
not staying out on the hill too long.
At about ten o'clock the night before,
I psych myself up by getting my skis in fantastic condition.
So when my head is on the pillow,
I've just been the closest I can be to ski racing.
And the next day I have that little bit of extra confidence,
knowing I have the best-prepared skis on the mountain.
All this time I'm letting the pressure
build up inside me
to where everything is ready to explode.
That's one of the places maturity comes in—
knowing yourself well enough so you know
just how you're going to respond in certain situations—
so that you can explode
exactly as the guy says "Go."

Billy Kidd

BY LOVE ALONE

It is love alone
whereby we are turned to God,
and changed into the form of God,
whereby we cleave to God
and are made one with God,
so that we are one spirit with him
and are beatified with him.

Martin Luther

GOD'S CONSOLATION

God can give you only one consolation,
and that is so to penetrate you,
so to fill you with his love,
that you must return to others again,
and become capable of loving them.
That is the kind of consolation
that God gives.
He makes you capable of wanting
to love the whole world.

Louis Evely

THE KINGDOM OF GOD

The Pharisees asked him,
"When will the kingdom of God come?"
He said, "You cannot tell by observation
when the kingdom of God comes.
There will be no saying,
'Look, here it is!'
or 'there it is!';
for in fact the kingdom of God
is among you."

Luke 17:20-21

TO SERVE GOD

We may serve God
by digging with our hands,
or by talking friendly
with our neighbor.

R. H. Benson

JESUS SPEAKS OF LIFE

I am the bread of life;
he who comes to me shall not hunger,
and he who believes in me shall never thirst.
But I said to you that you have seen me
and yet do not believe.
All that the Father gives me will come to me;
and him who comes to me I will not cast out.
For I have come down from heaven,
not to do my own will,
but the will of him who sent me;
and this is the will of him who sent me,
that I should lose nothing
of all that he has given me,
but raise it up at the last day.
For this is the will of my Father,
that every one who sees the Son and believes in him
should have eternal life;
and I will raise him up at the last day.

John 6:35-40

ONE WITH THE WEATHER

As soon as I was thoroughly wet through
on the way home,
I became one with the weather
and would not have changed the day.
It is only while one is dry
that one is out of sympathy with rain;
when one is wet through,
one minds it no more than trees do,
having become part of the day itself.

Edward Grey

ANOTHER DAY

I once liked to hunt, fish,
play chess, play musical instruments.
As I've gotten older,
these things have stopped challenging me.
I would rather work.
I cherish the hours in the morning
that I have to myself.
In the summer,
when I leave the house,
the sun is just beginning to rise.
The night has cleansed away
so many things,
and I am alive for another day.
I am given another day.
I am grateful.
I am humble.
It is beautiful, the dawn.
And I don't ask why,
any more than I would
if I saw a beautiful girl.

Michael De Bakey

THE GREATNESS OF GOD

As the marsh-hen secretly builds on the
    watery sod,
Behold I will build me a nest on the
    greatness of God:
I will fly in the greatness of God as the
    marsh-hen flies
In the freedom that fills all the space
    'twixt the marsh and the skies.

Sidney Lanier

INEFFABLE JOY

For the moment
nothing but an ineffable joy
and exaltation remained.
It is impossible fully
to describe the experience.
It was like the effect
of some great orchestra,
when all the separate notes
have melted into one swelling harmony,
that leaves the listener
conscious of nothing
save that his soul
is being wafted upwards
and almost bursting
with its own emotion.

William James

THE FATHER'S LOVE

We are God's children
and that means that we have a father in heaven
who knows us, cares for us, loves us.
He existed before all that is.
Our praise, thanks, and prayer
are only an echo which His love awakens in us.
See what kind of love
the Father has bestowed on us
that we should be children
not merely in name but in reality.

Adapted from *1 John 3:1*

THE JOY OF LOVE

We are often so solemn about love
that we forget love is a joy,
a thing to wonder at
and to laugh about.
I saw this joy one day recently
when I took my four-year-old niece
for a swim on one of our ocean beaches.
She stood, holding my hand for safety,
where the farthest reach of the thundering surf
would just touch her feet,
and she laughed aloud
at the sheer joy and fun
of all the noise and light and moving water.
She was loving life itself,
and all the new possibilities
life was offering to her—
the joy of wading in the surf,
the joy of shaping wet sand
into houses and castles,
the joy of discovering
quaint shapes and forms
in the driftwood
along the tideline.

David P. O'Neil

THE STRAWBERRIES

But we were after the best of the berries
the strawberries that grow in the deep woods.
Someone suddenly called out in front,
"Look there they are, and there's another lot"—
Joy of simplicity, of carrying!
The pattering of the first ones in the bucket.
But we had to submit to the young guide.
"Citizens, you just make me laugh,
we haven't got near the berries yet."
And then a clearing broke through the trees
with a drunkenness of berries, sunlight,
and flowers, it dazzled on our eyes,
it was one breathing Oh.
The strawberries were like a waking dream
their smell was terrifying. We ran
in among them with rattling pails,
and tripped, lay there drugged, using our lips
to pluck the big berries on their stems.

Yevtushenko

THE IMPERFECT EYE

I saw tonight that he is on my side,
the lion. For the first time, I saw it.
And by God all the furniture got up

and danced (that hulking desk
a creditable tango) and I, though not much
on my feet, waltzed through Judah

like a Crazy-priest. Sometimes joy
is like that, coming quick as dandelions
springing to attention while the sun

shudders still—a little—from the melting
winter. Anyway here I was with lions
to account for and that desk

and questionable antics all along
(indignities of sun and dandelions
while our bones still creak with Lent)

and I thought God, what now, until
again I heard the music of the dance
again I waltzed through Judah.

"I something fear my father's wrath" no more.

John L'Heureux

FLOWER IN THE CRANNIED WALL

Flower in the crannied wall,
I pluck you out of the crannies,
I hold you here, root and all, in my hand,
Little flower—but *if* I could understand
What you are, root and all, and all in all,
I should know what God and man is.

Alfred, Lord Tennyson

ALL THERE

Everything is symbolic,
everything is holy.
There is no special time
or place or person,
privileged to represent the rest.
And then democracy can begin.
The many are made one
when the totality is in every part.
When one thing is taken up,
all things are taken up with it;
one flower is the spring.
It is all there
all the time.

Norman O. Brown

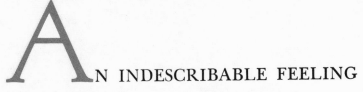

AN INDESCRIBABLE FEELING

I could only feel this perfectly when I was alone;
and then it would often make me shiver
from head to foot with the joy and fear of it,
when after being some time away from hills
I first got to the shore of a mountain river,
where the brown water circled among the pebbles,
or when I first saw the swell of distant land
against the sunset,
or the first low broken wall,
covered with mountain moss.
I cannot in the least describe the feeling;
but I do not think that this is my fault,
nor that of the English language,
for I am afraid no feeling is describable.
If we had to explain even the sense of bodily hunger
to a person who had never felt it,
we should be hard put to it for words;
and the joy in nature seemed to me
to come of a sort of heart-hunger,
satisfied with the presence of a Great and Holy Spirit.

John Ruskin

GROWING TOWARD GOD

THINGS BEYOND OUR IMAGINING, ALL PRE-pared by God for those who love him (1 Corinthians 2:9). ❦ Through faith, a person discovers God's presence within himself. Next he sees God's presence in other people. Finally he learns to recognize him in all the things of the world. Today perhaps the most exciting possibility for exploring the meaning of man in God lies in the future, in the shaping within the human creature through successive stages of development of a life really worthy of man's living. ❦ Growing toward God can have something of the experience of exploration. It is like traveling the roaring waves of the sea in search of a land. It involves holding fast to dreams. It involves straining after the promise of the truly mysterious, or is like traveling beyond tired mountains to touch with hands the loam of a hidden valley. More than that, it is like wanting to spin the wild universe in the palm of one's hand. ❦ People who feel exiled from the world as it is "make it clear that they are seeking . . . a better country" (Hebrews 11:4). ❦ They know that God is not ashamed to be called their God. He has blessed them for their hope and their endurance, and he is preparing a place for them: not only a heavenly place, but a new earth as well. All the earth is groaning in sympathy with mankind, as God sets free the bodies of men and women, making all of them his sons and daughters, that they might find a fuller resurrection. ❧ Those who are involved in a growth toward God are involved in the great experiment: Man. Restless to reach the wholly other, not content with the world of the present moment, they listen, as to a drummer's beat, to the steady pulse of the future. They understand something now of the springing shoots of corn, the promise of childhood, the spring latent in November, the sacred spirit hidden in the flesh. ❧ Fatigue and weariness may be their daily bread. Whispers in the crowd and threatening faces in the shadows may unsettle their strongest hopes. But within those who grow toward God there burns a strong eagerness. Maybe this is the familiar tension before the ascent. There is fear, but at the edge of discovery. There is concern, but it may transform the world. ❧ The believer's objective for the future is to create newness, to set free what is blocked up, to achieve the impossible; to alleviate suffering and renew humanity. People are free now, within the wide orbit of God's will, to choose, to determine, to decide their own final and noble condition.

LIKE DIVING IN

It is to me the most exciting moment—
when you have a blank canvas
and a big brush full of wet color,
and you plunge.
It is just like diving into a pond—
then you start to swim . . .
Once the instinct and intuition
get into the brush tip,
the picture *happens,*
if it is to be a picture at all.

D. H. Lawrence

THE ONLY REAL PROBLEM

Christian faith strains after the promises
of the universal future of Christ.
There is only one real problem in Christian theology:
the problem of the future.

Jürgen Moltmann

I AM WAITING

I am waiting for the Second Coming
and I am waiting
for a religious revival
to sweep thru the state of Arizona
and I am waiting
for the Grapes of Wrath to be stored
and I am waiting
for them to prove
that God is really American
and I am seriously waiting
for Billy Graham and Elvis Presley
to exchange roles seriously
and I am waiting
to see God on television
piped onto church altars
if only they can find
the right channel
to tune in on
and I am waiting
for the Last Supper to be served again
with a strange new appetizer
and I am perpetually waiting
a rebirth of wonder . . .

Lawrence Felinghetti

154

HIS PEOPLE

Thus says the Lord:
In a time of favor
I have answered you,
in a day of salvation
I have helped you;
I have kept you and given you
as a covenant to the people,
to establish the land,
to apportion the desolate heritages;
saying to the prisoners, "Come forth,"
to those who are in darkness, "Appear."
They shall feed along the ways,
on all bare heights shall be their pasture;
they shall not hunger or thirst,
neither scorching wind nor sun
shall smite them,
for he who has pity on them
will lead them,
and by springs of water
will guide them . . .

Isaiah 49:8-10

MAN AND THE SEED

The sky has its fire,
its waters, its stars,
its wandering electricity,
its winds, its fingers of cold.
The earth has its reddened body,
its invisible hot heart,
its inner waters and many juices
and unaccountable stuffs.
Between them all,
the little seed:
and also man,
like a seed that is busy and aware.
And from the heights and from the depths
man, the caller, calls.
Man, the knower, brings down the influences,
with his knowledge.
Man, so vulnerable, so subject,
and yet even in his vulnerability and subjection, a master,
commands the invisible influences and is obeyed.
He partakes in the springing of the corn,
in the rising and the budding
and rearing of the corn.
And when he eats his bread, at last,
he receives all he once sent forth,
and partakes again
of the energies he called to the corn,
from out of the wild universe.

D. H. Lawrence

MIRACLES

To me every hour of the light and dark is a miracle,
Every cubic inch of space is a miracle,
Every square yard of the surface of the earth is spread with the same,
Every foot of the interior swarms with the same.
To me the sea is a continual miracle,
The fishes that swim—the rocks—the motion of the waves—
the ships with men in them,
What stranger miracles are there?

Walt Whitman

A GIFT

But happy are your eyes because they see,
and your ears because they hear!
Many prophets and saints, I tell you,
desired to see what you now see,
yet never saw it;
to hear what you now hear,
yet never heard it.

Matthew 13:16-17

COMPARISONS

Who has measured the heavens
in the hollow of his hand
and marked off the heavens
with a span,
enclosed the dust of the earth
in a measure
and weighed the mountains
in scales
and the hills in a balance?
Who has directed the Spirit of the Lord,
or as his counselor has instructed him?
Whom did he consult for his enlightenment,
and who taught him the path of justice,
and taught him knowledge
and showed him the way of understanding?
Behold, the nations
are like a drop from the bucket,
and are accounted as the dust
on the scales;
behold, he takes up the isles
like fine dust.

Isaiah 40:12-15

WAITING

I wait for the Lord,
my soul waits,
and in his word I hope;
my soul waits for the Lord
more than for the morning . . .

O Israel, hope in the Lord!
For with the Lord
there is steadfast love,
and with him is plenteous redemption.

Psalm 130:5-7

A PRAYER FOR GENEROSITY

Lord, teach me to be generous.
Teach me to serve you as you deserve:
To give and not to count the cost;
To fight and not to heed the wounds;
To toil and not to seek for rest;
To labor and not ask for reward—
Save that of knowing
That I am doing your will.

Ignatius Loyola

Now

The next quarter of an hour
is of immeasurably greater importance
than eternal life,
and the conduct and content
of that quarter of an hour
is not helped but hindered
by thoughts and hopes of immortality.
Now is not a point of time.
It is all Time for us,
or more comprehensibly
the only part of time
in which action is possible.

Arthur Ponsonby

A HAPPENING

It is almost always
when things are all blocked up
and impossible
that a happening comes.
If you are sure you are looking and ready,
that is all you need.
God is turning the world around
all the time.

A. D. T. Whitney

A VISION OF A COMING

I had a strange thought this month
in the wind and snow.
A vision of the Coming—
not the Second Coming,
that dream of Christians,
but a coming of a man from the Arctic,
marching slowly down.
Brown, broad, majestic.
Great, flat-moon-shaped face.
Black eyes.
A pagan man to deliver us
from our stinking wars of religion,
wars of patriotism.
Our wars in which we use
the bodies of burned children
to ward off our childish nightmares
of a Communist world.
Our war for democracy
in which we blind, burn, starve,
and cripple children
so that they may vote at twenty-one.

Josephine W. Johnson

RICH—AND RESPONSIBLE

In comparison with the starving and the underdeveloped,
we are all rich, and therefore all responsible.
If I know that there are human creatures like me,
in some part of the world,
whose life is not worthy of man,
of a son of God,
who have neither house nor clothing,
neither food nor education,
then I must do all I possibly can
to help them,
to alleviate their suffering.

Helder Camara

THINKING TOGETHER

When "my" God becomes "our" God,
then something wonderful can happen.
"My" world becomes "our" world.
"My" life becomes "our" life.
Suddenly, we are alive together.
The alternative is, sadly,
that we may choose to be dead together.
The chips are down.
We are faced by either
a distinct possibility of annihilation
or a genuine promise
for the betterment of human life.
It is uniquely a time to sink or swim,
fish or cut bait,
die or face the truth about ourselves.
I find truth painfully beautiful.
It is the reservoir of hope.

Malcolm Boyd

A STATEMENT

Today we destroy Selective Service System files
because men need to be reminded
that property is not sacred.
Property belongs to the human scene
only if man does.
If anything tangible is sacred,
it is the gift of life and flesh,
flesh which is daily burned,
made homeless, butchered—
without tears or clamour from most Americans—
from Vietnam to Harlem to Watts—
wherever the poor live and die,
forgotten people,
the anonymous majority.

The Milwaukee Statement

THESE DAYS

These are not, however,
the days of miracles,
and I suppose it will be granted
that I am not to expect
a direct revelation.
I must study
the plain physical facts
of the case,
ascertain what is possible,
and learn
what appears
to be wise and right.

Abraham Lincoln

A PLACE WITH GOD

Let not your hearts be troubled;
you believe in God, believe also in me.
In my Father's house are many mansions;
if it were not so, I would have told you.
I go to prepare a place for you.
And . . . I will come again
and receive you unto myself,
that where I am, there you may be also.

John 14:1-3

A SELF-CREATING BEING

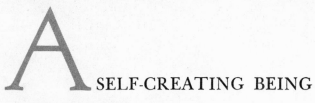

In Christian thought,
man is a free being before God,
a person subject to himself
and capable of freely determining
his own final condition.

Karl Rahner

WHO IS LIKE THE LORD?

Who is like the Lord our God,
who looks upon the heavens and the earth?
He raises the poor from the dust,
and lifts the needy from the ash heap,
to make them sit with princes,
with the princes of his people.
He gives the barren woman a home,
making her the joyous mother of children.
Praise the Lord!

Psalm 113:5-9

IDEAL AND REAL RELIGION

I have been speaking to you of religion at its best.
But an organized religion, a church,
is not a conventicle of saints.
It is like a net cast into the sea
that catches all sorts of fish . . .
So it is that, as generation follows generation,
there is always a gap between the ideal and the real,
between religion as it strives to be
and religion as it is in fact.
But apart from cases of self-deception or insincerity,
this gap or contrast does not imply
that religion is phony,
that religious people say one thing and do another.
The very being of man . . .

always is at best a striving.
The striving of the religious man
is to give himself to God
in something nearer the way
in which God has given himself to us.
Such a goal is always distant,
but it is not inhuman,
for it corresponds to the dynamic structure
of man's being,
to the restlessness that is ours
till we rest in God.

Bernard Lonergan

FREEDOM AND PRAYER

When once you have known what it is to be loved
    freely, submission no longer has any taste

All the prostrations in the world

Are not worth the beautiful upright attitude of a free
    man as he kneels. All the submission, all the
    dejection in the world

Are not equal in value to the soaring up point,
The beautiful straight soaring up of one single
    invocation
From a love that is free.

Charles Peguy

THE BISHOP'S WIDOW

I do not intend to stop anywhere
in this valley of grief,
but rather to walk steadily
on to the hills,
where new challenges
and opportunities await me.
I know God is there before me,
and I step into that open future
with faith that its meaning
and promise will unfold before me.
I need not look back.
There will be no pillars of salt,
no regrets.
Jim lives—and so do I.

Diane Kennedy Pike

THE COMING OF GOD HIMSELF

Christian hope is founded
not in social revolution
or wars of independence
but in the coming of God himself.
The sign of this hope
is anticipated in the church
in Word and sacrament.
This hope can and should become
the inexhaustible source
for social imagination
and for legal and political visions
in the name of freedom.

Jürgen Moltmann

PATIENCE

Be patient, my brothers,
until the Lord comes.
The farmer looking
for the precious crop
his land may yield
can only wait in patience,
until the winter
and spring rains
have fallen.
You too must
be patient
and stouthearted,
for the coming of the Lord
is near.

James 5:7-8

52

who are you, little i

(five or six years old)
peering from some high

window; at the gold

of november sunset

 (and feeling: that if day
has to become night

this is a beautiful way)

e. e. cummings

AND A NEW EARTH

For behold, I create new heavens
and a new earth;
and the former things
shall not be remembered
or come into mind.

But be glad and rejoice for ever
in that which I create;
for behold, I create
Jerusalem a rejoicing,
and her people a joy.

Isaiah 65:17-18

THE HUMAN ENTERPRISE

The human heart can go to the lengths of God.
Dark and cold we may be, but this
Is no winter now. The frozen misery
Of centuries breaks, cracks, begins to move;
The thunder is the thunder of the floes,
The thaw, the flood, the upstart Spring.
Thank God our time is now when wrong
Comes up to face us everywhere,
Never to leave us till we take
The longest stride of soul men ever took.
Affairs are now soul size.
The enterprise
Is exploration into God.

Christopher Fry

PERCEIVING GOD

What can be known about God
is plain to men,
because God has showed it to them.
Ever since the creation of the world
his invisible nature,
namely, his eternal power and deity,
has been clearly perceived
in the things that have been made.

Romans 1:19-20

AND SUDDENLY SUN

Through the caverns and heights and the slopes
  of the cities of man—
Through the cities that welcome the smells
  and the night and the rain—
Sweeps the mind of a father, the breath
  of a beautiful fire,
Burning and licking and stretching,
  impatient to spire
Life into shadowing heavenward
  skyscraper stone
Waiting for warmth and for light
  to be suddenly sun . . .

Alan Vincent